# A FAST APPROACH TO RAISING A HAPPY CHILD:

## A brief guide to successful parenting.

## Rebecca Smith.



### Table of content

# INTRODUCTION

Being a parent may be difficult. Kids have a way of pushing their parents to the brink in their tolerance and beyond, which leaves both discern and kid upset.

Raising a happy child means providing a secure, nurturing, and supportive surroundings that fosters their bodily, emotional, and social nicely-being. It also means putting limitations and supplying structure, at the same time additionally encouraging independence and self esteem. It means spending high-quality time collectively and fostering open verbal exchange, in addition to modeling positive conduct and inspiring healthy habits. It also gives support when needed and being willing to adapt and modify to meet the converting desires of children as they grow and develop. In the long run, raising a glad child requires assisting them increase a sense of motive, belonging, and connection to others, and the self assurance and abilities to navigate the demanding situations of lifestyles with resilience and charm.

Even as happiness might also appear pretty primary, one is both happy or now not. Many factors may contribute to your toddler's happiness. External stimuli, as an example, may additionally make your child glad (or, conversely, it is able to make your infant unhappy) (or, conversely, it may make your baby sad). When it comes to children , a touch making plans may additionally help. Right here are some of the matters you can do now to elevate a glad child.

# Chapter 1

Spend meaningful time with them

Among work and private commitments, the times skip us by means of within the blink of an eye fixed. Many parents are worried that they don't spend enough time with their kids, questioning if this may lead to developmental challenges. A few dad and mom experience lousy approximately operating complete time or fear about choosing to workout in the gym or go to dinner with buddies. Social media posts from live-at-home parents who can take their youngsters to the local zoo or work on colors and the alphabet with them best make contributions to this anxiousness.

But don't panic, Research shows the impact of the quantity and quality of time mothers spend with their youngsters has on the educational performance, behavior, and emotional well-being in their kids. This is not to minimize the need for time spent with kids, however as an alternative, to underline the concept that the exception of time is a great deal more vast than the amount of time. Kids deserve fantastic time with mothers and fathers or caregivers in general —that is what is most valuable to youngsters and what may also have an effective impact on them as they grow. It isn't approximately endless hours—it's approximately how you pick out to utilize that time.

Children are much less susceptible to face behavioral problems at home or school. Youngsters who're spending greater pleasant time with their households are less likely to participate in risky activities such as drug and alcohol usage.

Showing your youngsters that you love and care for them assists to preserve them mentally and emotionally resilient.

As a parent, the best approach to do this is to spend great time with them every day. Children who spend more pleasant time with their families are much more likely to be bodily healthy. Typically, spending great time together with your youngsters is essential to them, but is also critical to your well-being.

As parents or caregivers, we may additionally make picks to make sure time spent with our youngsters is extraordinary. Here are a few thoughts for busy families:

- Have a "connect" time every day together with your youngster. Do this face-to-face, if plausible; however if this isn't an option, broaden a pattern for doing so in other approaches, which include leaving a notice on your toddler's lunch bag, posting a message along with his toothbrush, or writing an encouraging announcement on a common whiteboard inside the home.

- Create a unique ordinary for you and your baby—something that may be achieved each day. For instance, let your youngster choose and read one book with you at bedtime.
- Beef up superb behavior. As an instance, if your teen completes his chores without your asking, acknowledge it with phrases of appreciation—even if you weren't opportuned to do so till the following day.
- Tell your youngster you appreciate him/her each day. And tell how vital he/she is to you and how he/she makes you feel.
- Make and enjoy food together with your kids every time you could.
- If time is limited, recall simple food that needs

very little time, or snatch a wholesome snack including an apple and sit for a few minutes and communicate along with your child. .

- Agenda time for doing an interest of your child's selecting. Be careful to comply with any kind venture without any interruptions.
- Play with your kids, regardless if it's at tub time or outdoor before you drop them off at preschool. Every tiny amount of time has a big effect!
- Be goofy together with your infant /children .

Turn off electronics even as you spend time along with your kid.

Instead of gifts, offer your kids your presence. One of the nicest matters to spend on your youngsters is your time. Children want to experience our devotion to them conveyed physically and vocally.

An extraordinary but often overlooked technique to selling proper behavior is absolutely to reward the moves you desire to peer.

# Chapter 2

Communication is crucial

As everyone who has interacted with a toddler can attest, handling children may be difficult. Whether it's a linguistic barrier among a discern and toddler, a war of wills between an authority discern and a child, or a easy misunderstanding among a teacher and adolescent, adult-infant conversation may be extraordinarily hard. Using essential strategies, but, you can not most effectively interact with kids but do it efficiently. It just needs listening, taking a hobby, setting limits, and gaining knowledge to compromise.

Communication does not show up in half of-hearted

grunts or fleeting sentences. To surely and efficiently communicate, set apart time for discussion, connection, or maybe absolutely informal communication, and watch your relationship increase.

If your own family has a lot happening, set apart 1-2 evenings a week for family dates, or one-on-one dates together with your kids.

Choose a time that doesn't interfere with different obligations. Set aside time that does not have other commitments or preceding plans, including an assembly or lesson.

Your cellphone, pc, or television is a distraction, and could no longer benefit you in speaking with children. While it's time to converse, do not allow this stuff within the room, or keep them. Flip off your smartphone, flip off your pc, and leave your tv aside.

In case you find cell telephones or computers are being specially complex to your circle of relatives' communique tries, set a rule to have no phones or computers out an hour before bed, or from dinner onward—then put in force the rule, and maintain yourself accountable.

If the kid in question is using a phone or the Internet and not listening at some point of class or whilst you are attempting to talk, kindly request that the phone is positioned away for the following 5 minutes.

Whether you're speaking or listening, create eye touch. Don't stare the child down, but ensure it is apparent that the child has your entire attention and attention. Don't glance across the room as they communicate, and don't look over their head whilst you communicate. Keep eye contact every time possible.

Blink as you normally would, peek down sometimes to see the child's arms as they speak, or their lips as it actions.

In case you can't keep eye contact, sit down so your eyes are on the identical degree,make sure you and the child are on equal footing.

Stay in the modern-day second. Don't permit your mind to wander while you are chatting or sitting with a teen. Keep your mind and eyes centered at the work at hand. Even if you are sitting comfortably in solitude, don't permit your thoughts to visit your to-do list—be aware of the kid's frame language, respiratory patterns, and silent verbal exchange.

Encourage kids to practice mindfulness with you. Lightly factor out if a toddler's attention has started to wander, or they have ended up less interested. Lead by example, and teach youngsters on how to be present.

Encourage your teenager of their interests, however do not force them to accomplish things. If a little one is interested in butterflies, consider a trip to the library to test out an e-book about butterflies. If a teenager is excited about politics, act a small, polite communique. If a youngster is head-over-heels for playing the oboe, inspire them to perform a mini-live performance for you.

There's a fine line between being concerned, and turning into overbearing. Ask how you may be engaged, and the way they could want you to be worried.

While a teenager communicates with you, especially about critical matters, repeat what they've said back to them, using your personal words, and following with, "correct ?" or "Do I understand ?" this would make the child recognise that you are listening however additionally provide them an opportunity to explain when you have misinterpreted what they've stated.

# Chapter 3

Set boundaries and discipline regularly

Powerful parents will develop clean limits and norms with

their children. In terms of practical parenting, consistency is the name of the game.

Continuously developing limits, delivering suitable consequences, and implementing the guidelines all day every day will be challenging. However, study what gets in the manner of being steady and take steps to increase your disciplinary consistency.

Set up residence policies so that you can frequently respond to undesired behavior. A written set of policies guarantees that youngsters are aware of what is anticipated of them. While you set up exceptions to the regulations, announce them beforehand.

This educates youngsters that there may be practical deviations to policies and which you're in charge of determining while such exceptions should take place.

Our youngsters analyze largely via modeling. Considering the fact that we can't break out from being an example to our children, pick out to be an excellent one.

Effective subject derives from the following. Get them efficiently, and you'll have significantly much less trouble together with your kids as they age due to the fact they've learnt the rules and what breaching them means.

1. CLARITY : Be unequivocal whilst you describe rights, norms, and barriers.

Don't expect your children to understand family rules until you've talked about them.

Be sure your youngsters recognize why these regulations are being imposed and the effects of violating the rules.

Involve your youngsters as lots as viable in formulating the regulations.

Try writing out your family regulations and posting them on the fridge.

2. CONSISTENCY: Be consistent in imposing regulations.

Keep on with the penalty that has been set for a damaged rule.

Discipline could be greater effective if your children had participated in developing the policies.

If a revision desires to be made to a family rule, speak about it earlier than the guideline is broken.

Be adaptive – as your kids mature, they're prepared for extra rights and revisions in regulations and bounds.

3. CONVERSATION : speak approximately rights, norms, and constraints regularly.

Be open to studying the fairness of regulation and the motives behind it.

Assist your youngsters learn how to speak with you about emotions.

Encourage your children to come to you once they want assistance.

Express recognition and agreement for your youngster together with your phrases, gestures, and tone of voice.

4. CARING : Use encouragement and support,

not simplest punishments for disobeyed guidelines.

Praise your children after they follow your own family policies, especially once they do what's requested of them without reminders from you.

While a rule is damaged, criticize the pastime and no longer your youngsters.

Comply with up swiftly whilst a rule is damaged; maintain calm and carry out the results your youngsters assume.

Ensure the punishments are ok for the damaged rule.

Admire your kids's rights, together with the right to privateness.

5. CREATE: Instill a sense of social responsibility in your children.

Allow your kids to realize you require ethical behavior, which includes honesty and fairness.

Set an instance of honesty, justice, and social responsibility to your kids to comply with.

# Chapter 4

## Help your youngster gain social skill

Learning social capabilities is a vital feature of toddler development. Suitable social talents help children to connect pleasantly with others and speak their desires, desires, and emotions efficiently. Plus, the advantages of excessive social abilities expand way past social interactions and acceptability. Kids with more social talents are probably to enjoy speedy advantages. As an instance, children having social capabilities may also lessen stress, for example, kids who are in daycare settings.

Social talents demand ongoing refinement as kids develop. They aren't things an infant both has or doesn't have. These talents keeps booming with age and may be taught and reinforced with attempt and practice.

Some social abilities are pretty complicated—like comprehending it is important to be assertive whilst a friend is being burdened or to stay quiet whilst you do not agree with a call from the umpire.

Search for instructional possibilities while you may aid your kids attain higher.

Make sure to rent your manners whilst you are coping with other people. Offer reminders whilst your kids fail to apply etiquette and congratulate them when you see them performing courteously.

There are various measures mothers and fathers might also take to enhance their child's social abilities:

1. Observe their interest

Enjoying others will come extra effectively when a teen is doing something they may be certainly interested in.

Whether it's partaking in a beloved recreation, playing an instrument they enjoy, or being part of an organization they may be interested in, this is step one towards strengthening social capabilities. It additionally puts a child with like-minded folks that would possibly ensure a more peaceful experience.

Even as it's vital so one can mingle with folks with various pastimes, beginning out with different kids who adore the identical gadgets is a brilliant technique to truly construct social skills.

2. Learn to Ask Questions

Once in a while when children are nervous or a dialogue slows, they may become greater reclusive and in the long run fail in future social conditions. In step with the center for improvement & gaining knowledge of, there are various strategies children can initiate and keep on high-quality discussions with others.

One key approach is to ask questions.

The finest method to discover others and create connections is to invite questions which might be particularly relevant to the individual the youngster is speaking to. Inspire your kids to invite questions that can't be answered with only a yes or no.

3. Practice Role Playing

Pretend-play, with both more youthful and older kids, is a amazing chance for children to actively increase their social abilities. LD on-line offers dads and moms sensible recommendations for powerful role-playing. Have your child pretend to be the man or woman they've hassle talking to or getting along with. This could come up with a feel of what this person is like, or as a minimum how your teen regards this specific man or woman.

4. Teach Empathy

If children have a more strong hold of how others feel, they may be substantially more likely to feel linked to different people and form healthy bonds. Parents advice teaching empathy by using speaking on several occasions with their children. Ask how other people would possibly sense when every of these items happens. Part of coaching empathy is to encourage youngsters to learn how to actively concentrate on others.

This takes being attentive to what others are pronouncing and then thinking about what the speaker has stated as soon as the talk is concluded.

5. Know Your Child's Limits

Some kids are actually more gregarious than others. A youngster that is hesitant and introverted ought to no longer be anticipated to engage inside the same way as a clearly gregarious child. Some kids are relaxed in huge conditions, at the same time as others discover it simpler to hook up with their friends while in smaller agencies. It's also critical to recognize a child's time limits. Younger children and people with particular desires may also only sense cozy socializing for an hour or two

6. Be an awesome role model

It is critical to be consciously aware of the way you have interaction with others while your youngster is watching. Are you asking queries of individuals after taking the time to actively concentrate? Do you express real empathy for friends and your own family in your existence?

Being an amazing model includes conscious work and forethought. Youngsters are usually watching the people in their lives.

It is essential to recognise that it'll take time on your kid to establish first-rate social capabilities. Social abilities are things which might be discovered and constructed upon throughout an entire life. In case your toddler appears to be suffering with social abilities greater than different kids, communicate to a healthcare specialist. At the same time as it may take a little additional reinforcement and maturity to catch up, a loss of social skills additionally is probably a symptom of other problems.

Kids with mental fitness problems like attention deficit hyperactivity disorder (ADHD) or autism may additionally fall disadvantaged socially. A health practitioner may additionally examine your child and decide if remedy is required to beautify social talents.

# Chapter 5

Tame your temper

Parents expect rage tantrums from 2 - 3-year-olds. But angry outbursts don't frequently halt beyond the toddler years. Older kids might have difficulties with fury and frustration too.

Some adolescents only lose their cool once in a while, while others seem to have a rougher time when things don't go their way. Kids who tend to have strong responses by nature would require more guidance from parents to regulate their tempers.

Controlling outbursts may be challenging for youngsters, and helping them learn to do so is a demanding responsibility for the parents who love them.

Try to be patient and cheerful, and realize that these abilities take time to develop and that just about any kid can progress with the correct coaching.

Managing kids may be a struggle. Some days retaining serenity while keeping your calm is challenging. But whether you're reacting to an occasional temper flare-up or a pattern of outbursts, managing your own emotions when things grow heated will make it easier to instruct adolescents to do the same.

To assist in regulating a temper, attempt to be your child's ally - you're both pushing to win over the anger that continues contributing to difficulties.

While your patience may be taxed by passionate outbursts, resistance, disobedience, fighting, and talking back, it's during these moments that you need your patience most. Of course, you feel irritated, but what is essential is how you control it.

Reacting to kids' meltdowns with shouting and outbursts of your own will simply encourage them to do the same (and is associated with an increase in children's poor behaviors). But retaining your calm and carefully coping with a demanding issue allows you to demonstrate and explain suitable techniques to handle wrath and annoyance.

Managing emotions and regulating behavior are talents that evolve consistently over time during infancy. Just like any other ability, your kids will need to acquire and practice them, with your instruction.

If it's unusual for your youngster to have a tantrum, when one does occur, clearly but gently restate the rules. Saying something like "I know you're angry, but no yelling and no name-calling, please" might be all your child needs to hear to recover control.

Then gently issue an instruction, such as "explain to me what you're angry about" or "please apologize to your siblings for bullying them." In this way, you're leading your child back to acceptable behavior and encouraging self-control.

Also, explain to your kid what will happen if they don't calm down — for example, "If you don't calm down, you will need to go to your room until you're able to stop screaming."

Kids whose temper outbursts are regular could lack the self-control essential to cope with irritation and rage and need greater support controlling those feelings.

# Chapter 6

Teach your child how to resist negative ideas

Be a positive-minded guardian, hold a ratio of five favorable reports for each one terrible. Extra compliance and super conduct will result.

Frequently kids who think badly have mothers and fathers who assume negatively. So the issue here is to restrain oneself from whining or moaning. In case you capture yourself grumbling or being critical . Just stop for a couple of minutes and take a deep breath.

If you could, attempt to make certain that everything which you say is positive, useful, kind and brings out the good in every scenario, I'm now not claiming it's going to be smooth.

But, if you want your teen to adjust their negative questioning habit, this could show them that it's achievable.

And also you'll be leading by using examples. Doing this may permit your kid to believe that there's an alternative method to doing things in an extra useful, realistic, and productive way.

Assist your youngster confront the unhappy, gloomy, or poor filter that they perceive matters with. Like altering the clear out in the front in their eyes.
You could enable them to notice that on the time their clear out is just letting out the awful. It's not their fault – it's just the manner they're viewing things. And they may exchange the filter out to permit for extra wonderful mind.
Help them observe things from numerous viewpoints. Appearance from specific angles of view. See if you could get useful resources that benefit your youngster to acquire new viewpoints. And you can explain that looking at matters in a different way might increase their self-esteem and self belief, help them get better from setbacks, and cope better with disappointments.
And they'll be thrilled! Tell your child a story about a scenario your kid normally feels awful about – such as

getting second in a race – and display how a child who thinks positively may additionally sense entirely in a different way approximately the same incident. Then ask 'which child is happier?' Ask them how individuals might feel if they concentrate on all the difficulties or disadvantages of the scenario, instead of concentrating on the beautiful factors.

Assist your child comprehend they'll be joyful if they imagine greater positive principles - Optimists are happier than pessimists

Some other option is to resource your youngster to set up a mind-set of gratitude. It has been proven that encouraging a youngster to write five matters they're grateful for every day complements their life delight, their happiness, and their grades in their education. Possibly they may write in a notebook at the stop of every day, things that they're pleased about or grateful for. Or whatever that went smoothly that day. Or make a long list of factors, and keep including the listing every time they think of recent things.

Overall, the most important thing is to show your child love and support, and to create a positive and nurturing environment for them to grow and develop.

www.ingramcontent.com/pod-product-compliance
Lightning Source LLC
LaVergne TN
LVHW020537160826
845677LV00015B/4122